NORTH AMERICAN DINOSAURS
TRICERATOPS

Marybeth Lorbiecki

Rourke
Publishing LLC
Vero Beach, Florida 32964

About The Author

Marybeth Lorbiecki has written over twenty books, and many of them have won awards. She loves to write about nature and wildlife. She and her husband, David Nataya, live in Hudson, Wisconsin with their three children—Nadja, Mirjana, and Dmitri.

www.rourkepublishing.com

Photos/Illustrations: Cover © Joe Tucciarone; title page and pages 6, 10, 15, 16, 18 © Hall Train Studios; page 4 © Davide Bonadonna; pages 8, 14 © Jan Sovak; page 12 © Francois Gohier; page 20 © The Field Museum; page 22 © Erik Omstevdt

Editor: Robert Stengard-Olliges

Cover and page design by Nicola Stratford

Library of Congress Cataloging-in-Publication Data

Lorbiecki, Marybeth.
   Triceratops / by Marybeth Lorbiecki.
      p. cm. -- (North American dinosaurs)
   Includes bibliographical references and index.
   ISBN 1-60044-253-6 (hardcover)
   ISBN 978-1-60044-335-0 (paperback)
   1. Triceratops--Juvenile literature. 2. Dinosaurs--North America--Juvenile literature. I.
Title. II. Series.
   QE862.O65L67 2007
   567.915'8--dc22
                              2006016259

Printed in the USA

CG/CG

Rourke Publishing

www.rourkepublishing.com – sales@rourkepublishing.com
Post Office Box 3328, Vero Beach, FL 32964

Table of Contents

"Three-Horned Face"

Huge feet pound. The earth shakes. A herd of dinosaurs stampedes. They are feisty and stocky and ready to fight. They are as large as African elephants and have heads like helmets, with three horns.

These dinosaurs are Triceratops. Triceratops means "three-horned face." One small horn sprouts over a beak-like mouth. Over each eye, a sharp spike longer than a golf club juts out.

The name Triceratops *means "three-horned face."*

These animals lived long, long ago near the Rocky Mountains. It was so long ago that no person was there to see them. The Rocky Mountains were very young. The mountains edged a saltwater sea. Triceratops ambled over the nearby hot, wet plains.

While *Triceratops* wandered the plains, other dinosaurs rambled through the woods. Turtles, frogs, and crocodiles slid into the waters. Fishes and swimming dinosaurs lived among them. Small mammals scurried around on the shores. But there were no dogs or cats, cougars or bears.

Roaming the Fern Prairie

When *Triceratops* roamed the prairies, the land was not covered with grass. These prairies were made of ferns and **cycads**, palm trees and flowering shrubs.

Triceratops had huge, powerful jaws. With its beak like a parrot's, it slashed through branches. It snapped tough fern stalks. Then its sharp back teeth cut the greens like scissors. New teeth were constantly growing in. Some adult dinosaurs had three rows of teeth on both sides!

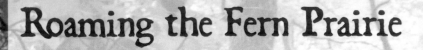

Scientists think *Triceratops* was an **herbivore**, eating only plants. *Triceratops* could use its horns to push down the trees and chomp the tops.

Triceratops was a plant eater. It used its horns to push down trees so it could eat the leaves.

Threat from T. rex

Stomping after *Triceratops* was *Tyrannosaurus rex*. *T. rex* was king. This dinosaur was the biggest of the Rocky Mountain meat eaters, or **carnivores**. *T. rex* could attack an injured or sick *Triceratops*.

It could catch a baby *Triceratops*, or an old one. Parts of *Triceratops* have been found in the fossilized **dung** of *T. rex*.

When *T. rex* came too near, a *Triceratops* herd may have charged. Or they may have grouped up and faced their horns out. Together, they'd be like a giant porcupine. *T. rex* would have to get dinner someplace else.

Tyrannosaurus rex *was an enemy of* Triceratops.

The Spear-Headed Fighters

When attacked, *Triceratops* thrust and charged with its horns. But it didn't use its horns much for jousting with *T. rex*. It used its horns mostly for fighting off other *Triceratops*. They clacked and locked horns, like deer and elk do. They probably fought over mates or **territory**. Many *Triceratops* bones show cracks and smacks.

The head of a *Triceratops* was almost one-third the size of its entire body. The bony

fan at the back was the frill. It wasn't as hard as armor.

Some *Triceratops* skulls have holes pierced in the frills.

The skin of *Triceratops* was bumpy and rough. The frill was probably brightly colored. These colors could attract a mate. The bigger the head and the brighter the frill, the easier it was to meet a mate.

Scientists know about dinosaurs because of clues they left behind. They left behind bones. They left behind eggs and dung. They left behind tracks in the mud.

Sometimes these remains hardened over time into rocks. Rock bones, eggs, tracks, and dung are called fossils. Scientists can tell many things from these fossils. They can tell that *Triceratops* lived about 72 to 65 million years ago. They can put the bones together to make a skeleton. Then they know how Triceratops' body was shaped. The fossilized dung shows what Triceratops ate.

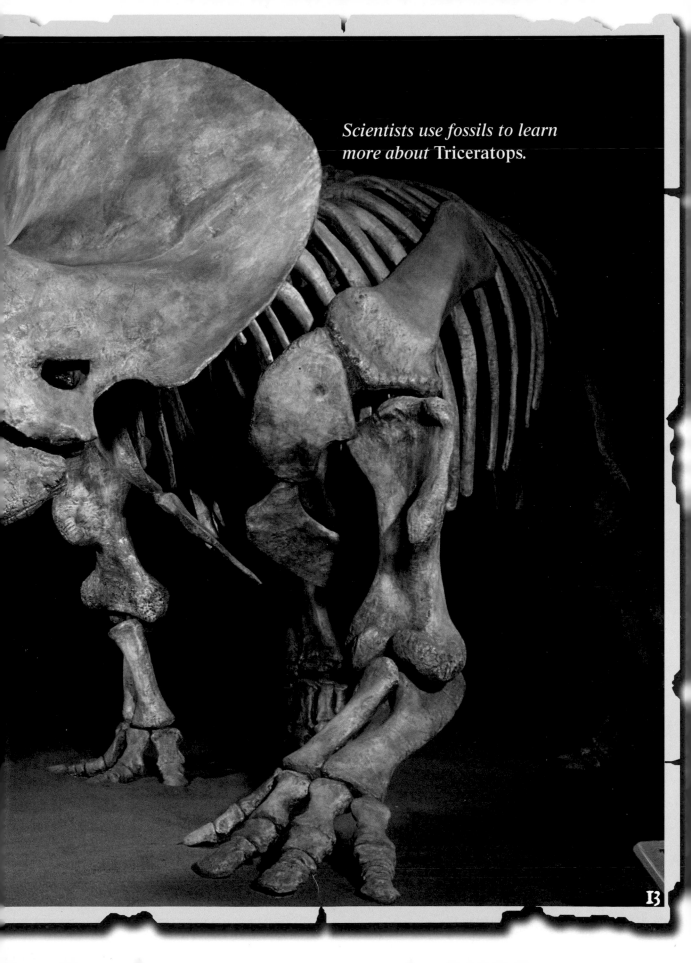

Scientists use fossils to learn more about Triceratops.

The bones of dinosaurs have growth rings inside. Scientists count the rings. This tells them the age of the dinosaurs when they died. Scientists use computers to compare the bones and tracks of dinosaurs to the muscles, bones, and tracks of animals alive now.

Triceratops had four flat toes and about a 20-inch (51 cm) wide footprint. It had five flat "fingers" on its front feet. It walked on all fours but could rear up on its back legs like an elephant. It may have also been able to lock its knees to sleep standing up, like horses do.

The tracks of *Triceratops* show it moved in herds like elephants. It moved slowly, but could probably run up to about 25 miles (40 km) an hour. It probably protected its young by keeping them in the middle of the herd.

The Hatchlings

Some dinosaur eggs have been found in nests. For this reason, scientists think that *Triceratops* laid its eggs in nests. The adults might have watched over the eggs.

After *Triceratops* hatched, it may have been ready to eat palms. Or it may not. At some point, a hatchling could eat on its own and join the herd.

Scientists do not know how this all happened. They do not even know if *Triceratops* was cold-blooded like lizards. Or was it warm-blooded like birds?

Chill Your Frill

Dinosaurs are related to both lizards and birds. Some dinosaurs, such as *T. rex*, have hips that look like those of lizards. Other dinosaurs have hips like birds. *Triceratops* had hips like birds.

Warm-blooded animals tend to have more blood vessels than cold-blooded animals. Scientists find many signs of a large amount of blood vessels on *Triceratops* skulls.

Triceratops may have used the vessels in its frill to cool off, the way elephants use their ears to cool off today.

One young boy in Montana was lucky enough to find a dinosaur. It was a new species: *Bambiraptor*. It looked a little like a bird. This discovery helped scientists see more clearly the connections between birds and dinosaurs.

Where Did They Go?

At one time, *Triceratops* was among the most numerous of the dinosaurs. Yet it died out. It was among the last dinosaurs to become **extinct**.

Some experts believe that the seasons grew too cold and icy. Other experts think that volcanoes erupted, or a gigantic boulder from space hit Earth. The skies might have turned black. The air would have been poisoned and the sunlight blocked. Plants probably died. Then dinosaurs that ate plants died. And the dinosaurs that ate other dinosaurs died.

No one knows exactly what happened. Scientists are still looking for clues. But they do know that *Triceratops* was one of the heaviest and toughest plant-eating dinosaurs ever.

Glossary

carnivore (KAR nuh vor) — animal that eats other animals

cycad (SYE ad) — large, hot-weather plant that has leaves like a palm or fern

dung (DUHNG) — animal feces

extinct (EK stingkt) — all members of a species have died out so no more will live

herbivore (HUR buh vor) — animal that eats plants

territory (ter uh TOR ee) — a large area of land

Index

Further Reading

Baker, Dr. Robert T. *Maximum Triceratops*.
    Random House, 2004.

Norma, David and Angela Milner. *Eyewitness Dinosaur*.
    DK Publishing, 2004.

Shatz, Dennis. *Fossil Detective Triceratops*.
    Silver Dolphin Books, 2005.

Websites to Visit

www.fieldmuseum.org/exhibits/exhibit_sites/dino/Triceratops1.htm

www.amnh.org/exhibitions/dinosaurs/display/horned.php

www.bhigr.com/pages/info/info_klsy.htm

www.nmnh.si.edu/paleo/dino/trinew.htm